A Guinea Pig Nutcracker

A GUINEA PIG
NUTCRACKER

BLOOMSBURY PUBLISHING
LONDON · OXFORD · NEW YORK · NEW DELHI · SYDNEY

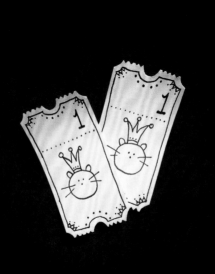

Dear members of the audience, please take your seats.
Tonight's performance of *The Nutcracker* is about to begin...

*The overture starts! Violins strike up a jaunty tune,
then dainty flutes and tinkling bells join in.*

The curtain rises on a festive scene.

Guests are arriving for an elegant Christmas Party at Clara's house. Full of excitement, little Clara dances towards the splendid tree to look at her presents.

Suddenly the music changes and a swaggering cello makes itself heard.

From nowhere, Clara's mysterious Godfather Drosselmeyer appears. He swirls around in his magnificent cape and hat, and hands Clara an enormous box tied up with ribbon.

Clara eagerly opens her present... but it isn't quite what she expected. Inside the box is a wooden Nutcracker, decorated like a little man in a red jacket.

Clara sticks a nut into the Nutcracker's mouth, raises his arm and – Crack! Crack! – he chews up the nut.

But Clara's reckless brother wants to play too and he snatches
the Nutcracker away.

Disaster strikes!

Clara rescues her beloved, broken Nutcracker and puts him back in his box. She whispers a gentle goodnight to him and turns to leave. Just then, the big clock strikes twelve.

Ting! Ting! Ting! Ting! Ting! Ting! Ting! Ting! Ting! Ting! Ting! Ting!

The double bass rumbles...

A terrifying figure spins in front of Clara. The Mouse King!

Violins and clarinets burst into a rousing call to arms.

Who will come to Clara's rescue? Yes, it's the wooden
Nutcracker! He jumps up and draws his sword.

Trumpets! Big drums! Crashing cymbals!

The Mouse King hurls himself at the wooden Nutcracker,
who fights valiantly against his whiskered foe. They thrust
and parry, dance and lunge.

In desperation, Clara pulls off a ballet slipper and flings it at the
Mouse King. It hits him on the head and knocks him out cold.

POUF!

As if by magic, the wooden Nutcracker has turned into a
handsome Prince.

The Nutcracker Prince smiles and takes Clara's hand. With a hop, skip and jump, everything changes.

A harp flutters and trumpets softly play.

Sweets, sweets, sweets as far as the eye can see...

Together, Clara and the Nutcracker Prince wander through a magical Christmas Forest in a dreamy *pas de deux*. They hear the faint harmony of angelic voices.

All at once, some beautiful Snowflakes prance into the glade. *Allegro!* They perform effortless pirouettes, their feet barely touching the ground.

The music changes and castanets begin to clatter joyfully.

The Land of Sweets is full of delightful characters. Here is Hot Chocolate, who curtsies to Clara and the Nutcracker Prince, then leaps into a *fandango**.

* This is a Spanish-style folk dance.

Two spectacular Candies dance into view, whirling around and around in a dizzying waltz. What a beautiful sight.

A trumpet sounds — violins swell — the flute plays a delicate melody...

The queen of the Land of Sweets appears: the heavenly, graceful Sugar Plum Fairy.

She begins to dance with gentle little steps.

She bends at the knee...

...before rising up on tiptoes for the *relevé*.

(There is much applause from all the other dancers.)

Clara claps along, delighted by the display.

Suddenly, inexplicably, she finds herself back at home.
But something magical still lingers in the air!

The brass begins again quietly, then swells to a glorious crescendo...

Was it all a dream?

And with that the stage goes dark, the velvet curtain falls and the orchestra plays its final chord.

The audience cheers and cheers until the curtain rises again and out steps the Sugar Plum Fairy, curtseying and waving. 'Bravo!' the audience cries. 'Bravo! Bravo!'

List of Performers

VIOLINIST . . . . *Sherlock*

CLARA . . . . *Ivy*

GODFATHER DROSSELMEYER . . . . *Elsie*

MOUSE KING . . . . *Teddie*

NUTCRACKER PRINCE . . . . *Poppy*

SNOWFLAKES . . . . *Marlin, Barry and Paul*

HOT CHOCOLATE . . . . *Mouse*

CANDIES . . . . *Doris and Doris*

SUGAR PLUM FAIRY . . . . *Bear*

Ivy

Poppy

Doris

Doris

Mouse

Bear

Marlin

Barry

Teddie

Paul

Elsie

Sherlock

The Ballet's History, in a Nutshell...

The story of Clara and the Nutcracker's adventures was first set
to music by the Russian composer Pyotr Ilyich Tchaikovsky in
the late nineteenth century. At the time, the ballet wasn't much
of a hit, but things started to change in 1940 when Walt Disney
featured part of the score in *Fantasia*. In this extraordinary film,
animated flower-fairies, mushrooms and even fish danced to the
music in their own way.

The Nutcracker began to make its comeback on stage in the years
that followed, and it became one of the most beloved ballets in the
world. It is now performed every December by both professional
and amateur dance companies, and it is quite impossible to imagine
the festive season without the swirl of tutus, the sound of violins
and a sprinkle of magic from the Sugar Plum Fairy.

Behind the Scenes

Tess Newall is a freelance set designer who specializes in fashion shoots and decorative painting. She carefully handcrafted all the miniature costumes and theatre sets that transformed a few normal guinea pigs into characters from *The Nutcracker*.

Phillip Beresford is a graphic designer and photographer. He used patience and skill to capture each scene on camera, and it is thanks to his excellent typographical instincts that the front cover features a font called 'Sugar Plum'.

Alex Goodwin is an editor and writer. He created this narrative of the ballet especially for the guinea pigs, basing their version of the story on Tchaikovsky's original score and the most popular productions from the past thirty years.

Thank You!

The publishers owe a huge, glittery thank you to Amanda
(F., R. and S.), Oliver, Pauline, Rebecca and Sophia; we're
also grateful to Alfred, Alice, Charles, Elizabeth, Evie,
Georgina, Isobel, John, Paul, Rosie and Steve.

Sharing the Love

Small pets are abandoned every day, but the lucky ones end up in rescue centres where they can be looked after and rehomed. You may not know it, but some of these centres are devoted entirely to guinea pigs. They work with welfare organizations to give first class advice and information, as well as finding happy new homes for the animals they look after. If you want to share a bit of sweetness this festive season, perhaps think of supporting your local rescue centre!

BLOOMSBURY PUBLISHING
Bloomsbury Publishing Plc
50 Bedford Square, London, WC1B 3DP, UK

BLOOMSBURY, BLOOMSBURY PUBLISHING and the Diana logo are trademarks of Bloomsbury Publishing Plc

First published in Great Britain 2019

A catalogue record for this book is available from the British Library

Library of Congress Cataloguing-in-Publication data has been applied for

ISBN UK : 978-1-5266-1332-5
ISBN U.S. : 978-1-63557-450-0

2 4 6 8 10 9 7 5 3 1

Costumes and props by Tess Newall
Photography and design by Phillip Beresford
Text by Alex Goodwin
Edited by Xa Shaw Stewart

Printed and bound in China by C&C Offset Printing Co., Ltd

All papers used by Bloomsbury Publishing Plc are natural, recyclable products made from wood grown in well-managed forests.
Our manufacturing processes conform to the environmental regulations of the country of origin

Guinea Pig Classics

The greatest stories. With added cuteness.

'These guinea pigs
really know how to act'
THE TIMES